Nine Months
Before You Were Born
I Loved You
First Time Mom Pregnancy Prayer Journal

This journal belongs to:

_____

_____

Due Date: _____ Birth Date:_____

Baby's Name:

_____

Weight: _____ Length: _____

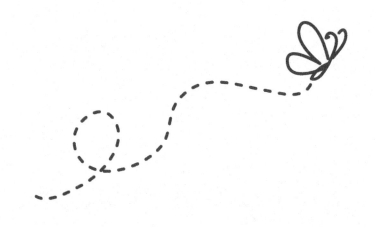

For this child I prayed:
and the Lord hath given
me my petition
which I asked of Him

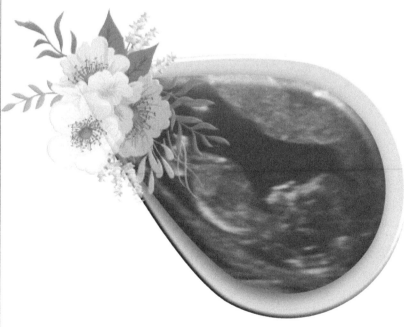

1 Samuel 1:27 KJV

Important Contact Info

Name		
Address		
City	State	Zip
Phone		
Email		

Name		
Address		
City	State	Zip
Phone		
Email		

Name		
Address		
City	State	Zip
Phone		
Email		

Name		
Address		
City	State	Zip
Phone		
Email		

Name		
Address		
City	State	Zip
Phone		
Email		

Name		
Address		
City	State	Zip
Phone		
Email		

Name		
Address		
City	State	Zip
Phone		
Email		

Name		
Address		
City	State	Zip
Phone		
Email		

Name		
Address		
City	State	Zip
Phone		
Email		

Our Birth Plan

Hospital:

Obstetrician:

Midwife:

Type of Birth:

Labor Coach(s):

Hospital Bag Contents:

- ☐ _____   ☐ _____
- ☐ _____   ☐ _____
- ☐ _____   ☐ _____
- ☐ _____   ☐ _____
- ☐ _____   ☐ _____
- ☐ _____   ☐ _____
- ☐ _____   ☐ _____
- ☐ _____   ☐ _____
- ☐ _____   ☐ _____

Registry Picks

gift item: store:

_____
_____
_____
_____
_____
_____
_____
_____
_____
_____
_____
_____
_____
_____
_____
_____
_____
_____
_____
_____
_____
_____
_____
_____
_____
_____
_____
_____
_____
_____
_____
_____
_____

Prenatal Appointments

Date	Provider	Time

Behold, children are a heritage from the Lord, the fruit of the womb a reward.

Psalm 127:3

Boy Baby Names

Girl Baby Names

1st Month

Notes & Reflections:

_____
_____
_____
_____
_____
_____

Initial wt: **Weight gain:**   **Belly circumference:**

Doctors Appointments, etc:

_____
_____

Sun	Mon	Tues	Wed	Thur	Fri	Sat

Date: _____

I thought about you today...

_____
_____
_____
_____
_____

My prayer for you today...

_____
_____
_____
_____
_____

Preparing for your arrival

My Hope for your Future

Date:_____

9 thought about you today...

_____
_____
_____
_____
_____

My prayer for you today...

_____
_____
_____
_____
_____
_____

Preparing for your arrival

My Hope for your Future

Date: _____

I thought about you today...

_____
_____
_____
_____
_____

My prayer for you today...

_____
_____
_____
_____
_____

_____

_____

_____

_____

_____

_____

_____

Preparing for your arrival

_____

_____

_____

_____

_____

My Hope for your Future

_____

_____

_____

_____

Date: _____

I thought about you today...

_____
_____
_____
_____
_____
_____

My prayer for you today...

_____
_____
_____
_____
_____
_____

My Hope for your Future

Date: _____

I thought about you today...

_____
_____
_____
_____
_____
_____

My prayer for you today...

_____
_____
_____
_____
_____
_____
_____

Preparing for your arrival

My Hope for your Future

Date:_____

I thought about you today...

_____
_____
_____
_____
_____

My prayer for you today...

_____
_____
_____
_____
_____
_____

Preparing for your arrival

My Hope for your Future

Date: _____

I thought about you today...

_____
_____
_____
_____
_____

My prayer for you today...

_____
_____
_____
_____
_____
_____

_____

_____

_____

_____

_____

_____

Preparing
for your
arrival

_____

_____

_____

_____

_____

_____

_____

My Hope
for your
Future

_____

_____

_____

_____

Date: _____

I thought about you today...

_____
_____
_____
_____
_____
_____

My prayer for you today...

_____
_____
_____
_____
_____
_____
_____

Preparing for your arrival

My Hope for your Future

Date: _____

I thought about you today...

_____
_____
_____
_____
_____
_____

My prayer for you today...

_____
_____
_____
_____
_____
_____
_____

Preparing
for your
arrival

My Hope
for your
Future

Date: _____

I thought about you today...

_____
_____
_____
_____
_____

My prayer for you today...

_____
_____
_____
_____
_____
_____

Preparing
for your
arrival

My Hope
for your
Future

2nd Month

Notes & Reflections:

_____
_____
_____
_____
_____
_____

Initial wt: Weight gain: Belly circumference:

Doctors Appointments, etc:

_____

Sun	Mon	Tues	Wed	Thur	Fri	Sat

Date:_____

I thought about you today...

_____
_____
_____
_____
_____

My prayer for you today...

_____
_____
_____
_____
_____

My Hope
for your
Future

Date: _____

I thought about you today...

_____
_____
_____
_____
_____

My prayer for you today...

_____
_____
_____
_____
_____

Preparing for your arrival

My Hope for your Future

Date: _____

I thought about you today...

_____
_____
_____
_____
_____
_____

My prayer for you today...

_____
_____
_____
_____
_____
_____
_____

My Hope
for your
Future

Date: _____

I thought about you today...

_____
_____
_____
_____
_____

My prayer for you today...

_____
_____
_____
_____
_____
_____

Preparing for your arrival

My Hope for your Future

Date:_____

I thought about you today...

_____
_____
_____
_____
_____
_____

My prayer for you today...

_____
_____
_____
_____
_____
_____

Preparing for your arrival

My Hope for your Future

Date: _____

I thought about you today...

_____
_____
_____
_____
_____

My prayer for you today...

_____
_____
_____
_____
_____
_____

Preparing for your arrival

My Hope for your Future

Date: _____

I thought about you today...

_____
_____
_____
_____
_____
_____

My prayer for you today...

_____
_____
_____
_____
_____
_____
_____

Preparing for your arrival

My Hope for your Future

Date: _____

I thought about you today...

_____

_____

_____

_____

_____

My prayer for you today...

_____

_____

_____

_____

_____

_____

Preparing
for your
arrival

My Hope
for your
Future

Date: _____

I thought about you today...

_____
_____
_____
_____
_____

My prayer for you today...

_____
_____
_____
_____
_____
_____

Preparing
for your
arrival

My Hope
for your
Future

Date:_____

I thought about you today...

_____
_____
_____
_____
_____
_____

My prayer for you today...

_____
_____
_____
_____
_____
_____

Preparing for your arrival

My Hope for your Future

3rd Month

Notes & Reflections:

_____
_____
_____
_____
_____
_____
_____

Initial wt: **Weight gain:**   **Belly circumference:**

Doctors Appointments, etc:

_____
_____

Sun	Mon	Tues	Wed	Thur	Fri	Sat

Date: _____

I thought about you today...

_____
_____
_____
_____
_____
_____

My prayer for you today...

_____
_____
_____
_____
_____
_____

_____

_____

_____

_____

_____

Preparing
for your
arrival

_____

_____

_____

_____

_____

_____

My Hope
for your
Future

_____

_____

_____

_____

_____

Date:_____

I thought about you today...

_____
_____
_____
_____
_____
_____

My prayer for you today...

_____
_____
_____
_____
_____
_____
_____

Preparing for your arrival

My Hope for your Future

Date:_____

I thought about you today...

_____
_____
_____
_____
_____
_____
_____

My prayer for you today...

_____
_____
_____
_____
_____
_____
_____

Preparing for your arrival

My Hope for your Future

Date: _____

I thought about you today...

_____
_____
_____
_____
_____
_____

My prayer for you today...

_____
_____
_____
_____
_____
_____

Preparing for your arrival

My Hope for your Future

Date: _____

I thought about you today...

_____
_____
_____
_____
_____

My prayer for you today...

_____
_____
_____
_____
_____

Date:_____

I thought about you today...

_____
_____
_____
_____
_____
_____

My prayer for you today...

_____
_____
_____
_____
_____
_____

Preparing for your arrival

My Hope for your Future

Date: _____

I thought about you today...

_____
_____
_____
_____
_____
_____

My prayer for you today...

_____
_____
_____
_____
_____
_____

Preparing for your arrival

My Hope for your Future

Date: _____

I thought about you today...

_____

_____

_____

_____

_____

My prayer for you today...

_____

_____

_____

_____

_____

_____

Preparing for your arrival

My Hope for your Future

Date: _____

I thought about you today...

_____
_____
_____
_____
_____
_____

My prayer for you today...

_____
_____
_____
_____
_____
_____
_____

My Hope
for your
Future

Date: _____

9 thought about you today...

_____
_____
_____
_____
_____
_____

My prayer for you today...

_____
_____
_____
_____
_____
_____

4th Month

Notes & Reflections:

_____
_____
_____
_____
_____
_____
_____

Initial wt: Weight gain: Belly circumference:

Doctors Appointments, etc:
_____
_____

Sun	Mon	Tues	Wed	Thur	Fri	Sat

Our family will soon grow by 1.

It's a ...

_____!

Date: _____

I thought about you today...

_____
_____
_____
_____
_____
_____

My prayer for you today...

_____
_____
_____
_____
_____
_____

Place Sonogram
Or Photo Here

Date: _____

I thought about you today...

_____
_____
_____
_____
_____

My prayer for you today...

_____
_____
_____
_____
_____
_____

Preparing
for your
arrival

My Hope
for your
Future

Date: _____

I thought about you today...

_____
_____
_____
_____
_____

My prayer for you today...

_____
_____
_____
_____
_____
_____

_Preparing
for your
arrival_

_My Hope
for your
Future_

Date: _____

I thought about you today...

_____

_____

_____

_____

_____

My prayer for you today...

_____

_____

_____

_____

_____

_Preparing
for your
arrival_

_My Hope
for your
Future_

Date: _____

I thought about you today...

_____
_____
_____
_____
_____
_____

My prayer for you today...

_____
_____
_____
_____
_____
_____
_____

Preparing for your arrival

My Hope for your Future

Date: _____

I thought about you today...

_____
_____
_____
_____
_____

My prayer for you today...

_____
_____
_____
_____
_____

My Hope
for your
Future

Date:_____

I thought about you today...

_____
_____
_____
_____
_____

My prayer for you today...

_____
_____
_____
_____
_____

Preparing for your arrival

My Hope for your Future

Date: _____

I thought about you today...

_____
_____
_____
_____
_____

My prayer for you today...

_____
_____
_____
_____
_____

Preparing for your arrival

My Hope for your Future

Date:_____

I thought about you today...

_____
_____
_____
_____
_____

My prayer for you today...

_____
_____
_____
_____
_____

Preparing for your arrival

My Hope for your Future

Date:_____

I thought about you today...

_____
_____
_____
_____
_____
_____

My prayer for you today...

_____
_____
_____
_____
_____
_____
_____

Preparing for your arrival

My Hope for your Future

5th Month

Notes & Reflections:

_____
_____
_____
_____
_____
_____

Initial wt: Weight gain: Belly circumference:

Doctors Appointments, etc:

_____
_____

Sun	Mon	Tues	Wed	Thur	Fri	Sat

Date: _____

I thought about you today...

_____
_____
_____
_____
_____
_____

My prayer for you today...

_____
_____
_____
_____
_____
_____

My Hope

for your

Future

Date: _____

I thought about you today...

_____
_____
_____
_____
_____

My prayer for you today...

_____
_____
_____
_____
_____

Preparing
for your
arrival

My Hope
for your
Future

Date: _____

I thought about you today...

_____
_____
_____
_____
_____
_____

My prayer for you today...

_____
_____
_____
_____
_____
_____

My Hope
for your
Future

Date: _____

I thought about you today...

_____
_____
_____
_____
_____

My prayer for you today...

_____
_____
_____
_____
_____

Preparing for your arrival

My Hope for your Future

Date: _____

I thought about you today...

_____

_____

_____

_____

_____

My prayer for you today...

_____

_____

_____

_____

_____

_____

_____

_____

_____

_____

_____

_____

Preparing for your arrival

_____

_____

_____

_____

_____

My Hope for your Future

_____

_____

_____

_____

_____

Date: _____

I thought about you today...

_____
_____
_____
_____
_____
_____

My prayer for you today...

_____
_____
_____
_____
_____
_____
_____

Preparing
for your
arrival

My Hope
for your
Future

Date: _____

I thought about you today...

_____
_____
_____
_____
_____

My prayer for you today...

_____
_____
_____
_____
_____
_____

Preparing for your arrival

My Hope for your Future

Date: _____

I thought about you today...

_____
_____
_____
_____
_____
_____

My prayer for you today...

_____
_____
_____
_____
_____
_____
_____

*Preparing
for your
arrival*

*My Hope
for your
Future*

Date: _____

I thought about you today...

_____
_____
_____
_____
_____

My prayer for you today...

_____
_____
_____
_____
_____
_____

My Hope
for your
Future

Date:_____

I thought about you today...

_____
_____
_____
_____
_____
_____

My prayer for you today...

_____
_____
_____
_____
_____
_____
_____

Preparing for your arrival

My Hope for your Future

6th Month

Notes & Reflections:

_____
_____
_____
_____
_____
_____
_____

Initial wt: Weight gain: Belly circumference:

Doctors Appointments, etc:

_____
_____

Sun	Mon	Tues	Wed	Thur	Fri	Sat

Date:_____

I thought about you today...

_____
_____
_____
_____
_____

My prayer for you today...

_____
_____
_____
_____
_____
_____

Preparing for your arrival

My Hope for your Future

Date: _____

I thought about you today...

_____
_____
_____
_____
_____

My prayer for you today...

_____
_____
_____
_____
_____
_____

My Hope
for your
Future

Date: _____

I thought about you today...

_____
_____
_____
_____
_____

My prayer for you today...

_____
_____
_____
_____
_____
_____

Preparing for your arrival

My Hope for your Future

Date: _____

I thought about you today...

_____
_____
_____
_____
_____

My prayer for you today...

_____
_____
_____
_____
_____

_____

_____

_____

_____

_____

Preparing for your arrival

_____

_____

_____

_____

_____

My Hope for your Future

_____

_____

_____

Date: _____

I thought about you today...

_____
_____
_____
_____
_____
_____

My prayer for you today...

_____
_____
_____
_____
_____
_____

Preparing for your arrival

My Hope for your Future

Date: _____

I thought about you today...

_____
_____
_____
_____
_____

My prayer for you today...

_____
_____
_____
_____
_____
_____

_____

_____

_____

_____

_____

_____

_____

Preparing for your arrival

_____

_____

_____

_____

_____

My Hope for your Future

_____

_____

_____

_____

Date:_____

I thought about you today...

_____
_____
_____
_____
_____
_____

My prayer for you today...

_____
_____
_____
_____
_____
_____
_____

Preparing
for your
arrival

My Hope
for your
Future

Date: _____

I thought about you today...

_____
_____
_____
_____
_____

My prayer for you today...

_____
_____
_____
_____
_____

Preparing
for your
arrival

My Hope
for your
Future

Date: _____

I thought about you today...

_____
_____
_____
_____
_____

My prayer for you today...

_____
_____
_____
_____
_____

Preparing
for your
arrival

My Hope
for your
Future

Date: _____

I thought about you today...

_____
_____
_____
_____
_____

My prayer for you today...

_____
_____
_____
_____
_____

_____

_____

_____

_____

_____

_____

_____

_____

Preparing for your arrival

My Hope for your Future

_____

_____

_____

_____

_____

_____

_____

7th Month

Notes & Reflections:

_____
_____
_____
_____
_____
_____
_____

Initial wt: **Weight gain:**   **Belly circumference:**

Doctors Appointments, etc:

_____
_____

Sun	Mon	Tues	Wed	Thur	Fri	Sat

Date:_____

I thought about you today...

_____
_____
_____
_____
_____

My prayer for you today...

_____
_____
_____
_____
_____

_____

_____

_____

_____

_____

_____

_____

Preparing for your arrival

_____

_____

_____

_____

_____

My Hope for your Future

_____

_____

_____

_____

Date: _____

I thought about you today...

_____
_____
_____
_____
_____
_____

My prayer for you today...

_____
_____
_____
_____
_____
_____

My Hope

for your

Future

Date: _____

I thought about you today...

_____
_____
_____
_____
_____

My prayer for you today...

_____
_____
_____
_____
_____

My Hope
for your
Future

Date:_____

I thought about you today...

_____
_____
_____
_____
_____
_____

My prayer for you today...

_____
_____
_____
_____
_____
_____

My Hope
for your
Future

Date: _____

I thought about you today...

_____
_____
_____
_____
_____

My prayer for you today...

_____
_____
_____
_____
_____
_____

My Hope

for your

Future

Date:_____

I thought about you today...

_____
_____
_____
_____
_____
_____

My prayer for you today...

_____
_____
_____
_____
_____
_____

Preparing for your arrival

My Hope for your Future

Date: _____

I thought about you today...

_____
_____
_____
_____
_____
_____

My prayer for you today...

_____
_____
_____
_____
_____
_____
_____

Preparing for your arrival

My Hope for your Future

Date: _____

I thought about you today...

_____
_____
_____
_____
_____
_____
_____

My prayer for you today...

_____
_____
_____
_____
_____
_____
_____

_____

_____

_____

_____

_____

_____

Preparing
for your
arrival

_____

_____

_____

_____

_____

My Hope
for your
Future

_____

_____

_____

_____

Date: _____

9 thought about you today...

_____
_____
_____
_____
_____
_____

My prayer for you today...

_____
_____
_____
_____
_____
_____

Preparing for your arrival

My Hope for your Future

Date:_____

I thought about you today...

_____
_____
_____
_____
_____
_____

My prayer for you today...

_____
_____
_____
_____
_____
_____

Preparing
for your
arrival

My Hope
for your
Future

8th Month

Notes & Reflections:

_____
_____
_____
_____
_____
_____
_____

Initial wt: Weight gain: Belly circumference:

Doctors Appointments, etc:

_____
_____

Sun	Mon	Tues	Wed	Thur	Fri	Sat

Baby Shower Gifts

Gift	Giver

Date: _____

I thought about you today...

_____
_____
_____
_____
_____
_____

My prayer for you today...

_____
_____
_____
_____
_____
_____

_____

_____

_____

_____

_____

_____

_____

Preparing for your arrival

_____

My Hope for your Future

_____

_____

_____

_____

_____

Date: _____

I thought about you today...

_____
_____
_____
_____
_____

My prayer for you today...

_____
_____
_____
_____
_____
_____

Preparing for your arrival

My Hope for your Future

Date: _____

I thought about you today...

_____

_____

_____

_____

_____

My prayer for you today...

_____

_____

_____

_____

_____

_____

Preparing for your arrival

My Hope for your Future

Date: _____

I thought about you today...

_____
_____
_____
_____
_____

My prayer for you today...

_____
_____
_____
_____
_____

_____

_____

_____

_____

Preparing
for your
arrival

_____

_____

_____

_____

My Hope
for your
Future

_____

_____

Date:_____

I thought about you today...

_____
_____
_____
_____
_____
_____

My prayer for you today...

_____
_____
_____
_____
_____
_____

Preparing for your arrival

My Hope for your Future

Date: _____

I thought about you today...

_____
_____
_____
_____
_____

My prayer for you today...

_____
_____
_____
_____
_____
_____

_____

_____

_____

_____

_____

_____

_____

Preparing
for your
arrival

_____

_____

_____

_____

_____

My Hope
for your
Future

_____

_____

_____

_____

Date:_____

I thought about you today...

_____
_____
_____
_____
_____

My prayer for you today...

_____
_____
_____
_____
_____
_____

Preparing for your arrival

My Hope for your Future

Date: _____

I thought about you today...

_____
_____
_____
_____
_____
_____

My prayer for you today...

_____
_____
_____
_____
_____
_____

_____

_____

_____

_____

_____

Preparing for your arrival

_____

_____

_____

_____

_____

My Hope for your Future

_____

_____

_____

_____

Date:_____

I thought about you today...

_____
_____
_____
_____
_____
_____

My prayer for you today...

_____
_____
_____
_____
_____
_____
_____

Preparing for your arrival

My Hope for your Future

Date: _____

I thought about you today...

_____
_____
_____
_____
_____

My prayer for you today...

_____
_____
_____
_____
_____

Preparing for your arrival

My Hope for your Future

9th Month

Notes & Reflections:

_____

_____

_____

_____

_____

_____

_____

Initial wt: **Weight gain:**   **Belly circumference:**

Doctors Appointments, etc:

_____

_____

Sun	Mon	Tues	Wed	Thur	Fri	Sat

We welcomed our bouncing

Baby_____ at _____am/pm

On _____20___.

Baby weighed in at _____lbs___oz,

And was _____inches long.

Happy

Birthday!

_____

BABY'S NAME

Date: _____

I thought about you today...

_____
_____
_____
_____
_____

My prayer for you today...

_____
_____
_____
_____
_____

Preparing for your arrival

My Hope for your Future

Date: _____

I thought about you today...

_____
_____
_____
_____
_____
_____

My prayer for you today...

_____
_____
_____
_____
_____
_____
_____

Preparing for your arrival

My Hope for your Future

Date:_____

I thought about you today...

_____
_____
_____
_____
_____

My prayer for you today...

_____
_____
_____
_____
_____

Preparing for your arrival

My Hope for your Future

Date: _____

I thought about you today...

_____
_____
_____
_____
_____
_____

My prayer for you today...

_____
_____
_____
_____
_____
_____
_____

Preparing
for your
arrival

My Hope
for your
Future

Date: _____

I thought about you today...

_____
_____
_____
_____
_____

My prayer for you today...

_____
_____
_____
_____
_____
_____

Date:_____

I thought about you today...

_____
_____
_____
_____
_____

My prayer for you today...

_____
_____
_____
_____
_____

Date:_____

I thought about you today...

_____
_____
_____
_____
_____

My prayer for you today...

_____
_____
_____
_____
_____

Preparing for your arrival

My Hope for your Future

Date: _____

I thought about you today...

_____
_____
_____
_____
_____

My prayer for you today...

_____
_____
_____
_____
_____
_____

Preparing
for your
arrival

My Hope
for your
Future

Date: _____

I thought about you today...

_____
_____
_____
_____
_____
_____

My prayer for you today...

_____
_____
_____
_____
_____
_____

Preparing for your arrival

My Hope for your Future

Date:_____

I thought about you today...

_____
_____
_____
_____
_____

My prayer for you today...

_____
_____
_____
_____
_____

Place Photo Here

A Lullaby

The stars are twinkling in the skies,

The earth is lost in slumbers deep;

So hush, my sweet, and close thine eyes

And let me lull thy soul to sleep.

Compose thy dimpled hands to rest,

And like a little birdling lie

Secure within thy cozy nest

Upon my loving mother breast

And slumber to my lullaby.

So hushaby-O hushaby.

Eugene Fields

Thank you for your purchase. We are truly grateful for your support. Our goal is to produce aesthetically pleasing and practical products that, in some small way, make your days better.

Your satisfaction is important to us. Please return to your order history on Amazon, and share your honest opinion.

Thanks again,

Samantha Romans

Made in the USA
Coppell, TX
08 July 2022

79705542R00118